IRISH
AND
PROUD
OF IT

summersdale

IRISH AND PROUD OF IT

This edition copyright © Summersdale Publishers Ltd, 2021
First published in 2014

Original text by Malcolm Croft, updated by Miranda Moore

All rights reserved.

No part of this book may be reproduced by any means, nor transmitted, nor translated into a machine language, without the written permission of the publishers.

Condition of Sale
This book is sold subject to the condition that it shall not, by way of trade or otherwise, be lent, resold, hired out or otherwise circulated in any form of binding or cover other than that in which it is published and without a similar condition including this condition being imposed on the subsequent purchaser.

An Hachette UK Company
www.hachette.co.uk

Summersdale Publishers Ltd
Part of Octopus Publishing Group Limited
Carmelite House
50 Victoria Embankment
LONDON
EC4Y 0DZ
UK

www.summersdale.com

Printed and bound in China

ISBN: 978-1-78783-650-1

Substantial discounts on bulk quantities of Summersdale books are available to corporations, professional associations and other organizations. For details contact general enquiries: telephone: +44 (0) 1243 771107 or email: enquiries@summersdale.com.

CONTENTS

May you have the
hindsight to know where
you have been, the
foresight to know where
you are going, and the
insight to know when you
have gone too far.

IRISH BLESSING

INTRODUCTION

Dia duit!

If you're Irish, you're Irish, wherever you are in the world. We may be a small nation, but we're big in personality and we take enormous pride in all our global compatriots, united as we are in our heritage.

This little book will take you on a tour of everything that makes our great country beautiful. Add to that the culture, the craic, and a pint or two of that black stout, and we have much to celebrate.

So join us on a magical journey to discover what makes people Irish … and proud of it!

MAKING
HISTORY

Important Dates
in Our History

The earliest known humans in Ireland can be traced to around **10,500** BC, as evidenced by a bear bone found in County Clare with visible signs of butchering. After that, hunter-gatherers are known to have been roaming Ireland by around 7500 BC, with agriculture emerging some 3,500 years later. Celtic tribes settled in Ireland in the first millennium BC and brought with them the language and culture that was to influence Irish life and society thereafter.

St Patrick's Day on March 17 is no longer just a national holiday and feast day in Ireland—the entire western world now celebrates the life of Ireland's most beloved saint, the man who brought Christianity to the island around 430 BC. A popular toast to St Patrick on this special day is this:

May the roof above you never fall in, and those gathered beneath it never fall out.

**OUR GREATEST GLORY
IS NOT IN NEVER FALLING,
BUT IN RISING EVERY
TIME WE FALL.**

Oliver Goldsmith

In **October 1171**, Henry Plantagenet (King Henry II of England) invaded Ireland and established the island as an English colony, the "Lordship of Ireland." The Lordship survived almost 400 turbulent years—enduring successive famines, a Scots uprising, the Black Death, and an indigenous Irish resurgence—until Henry VIII proclaimed himself king in 1542, formally uniting England and Ireland under one crown.

The momentous Battle of the Boyne in **1690** was an important engagement that was to influence the religious beliefs of the nation up to the present day. War had broken out between the two rival claimants to the thrones of England, Ireland and Scotland, Catholic King James II and Protestant King William III. They clashed at the River Boyne, near Drogheda on the east coast. William won the battle and James returned to exile in France, his hopes of regaining his former powers crushed.

I'M IRISH.
WE THINK
SIDEWAYS.

SPIKE MILLIGAN

One of the most tragic
and controversial events in
Irish history was the Great Famine
of **1845–1849**. Over a million Irish
people starved to death after a potato
blight wiped out 90 percent of the
country's main food staple, while other
foods were shipped out to England. Huge
numbers of those who tried to emigrate
to England, Canada, and the US died
in transit due to the appalling
conditions on board
the vessels.

The **Easter Rising** was launched by Irish
republicans in **April 1916** to end British
rule and bring about an independent
Irish Republic. Of the 485 people killed
during six days of fighting, 70 percent
were Irish, many of them civilians, and
parts of central Dublin were rebuilt
following shelling of rebel positions
by British armed forces. After 16 of the
Rising's leaders were executed by the
British in May 1916, popular support for
Irish independence surged, resulting in
the establishment of the Irish Free State
in **1922**.

EVEN WHEN THEY
HAVE NOTHING,
THE IRISH EMIT A KIND
OF HAPPINESS, A JOY.

Fiona Shaw

The Republic of Ireland Act of **1948** was signed into law by the Irish parliament on December 21 that year. It was the day that 26 counties of Ireland declared themselves the Irish Republic, free from British control. In the Ireland Act of the following year, Britain declared that Northern Ireland would remain a part of the UK unless the Parliament of Northern Ireland formally expressed a wish to join a united Ireland.

There are only
two kinds of people
in the world: the Irish
and those who wish
they were.

IRISH SAYING

April 10, 1998 marks the day the Good Friday Agreement was signed— an important step in the peace process and an end to the Troubles in Northern Ireland. Some of the major figures party to the agreement were British Prime Minister Tony Blair, Sinn Féin leader Gerry Adams, David Trimble (soon to be appointed First Minister of Northern Ireland), Martin McGuinness (later appointed deputy First Minister of Northern Ireland), John Hume (leader of the Social Democratic and Labour Party), Northern Ireland Secretary Mo Mowlam, and the Taoiseach, Bertie Ahern.

**WHEREVER YOU GO
AND WHATEVER YOU DO,
MAY THE LUCK OF THE IRISH
BE THERE WITH YOU.**

Irish proverb

On **January 1, 2007**, Irish became one of the 24 official languages of the European Union. The national first language of Ireland, it continues to be taught in Irish schools and has no direct words for "yes" and "no." Irish has no letters j, k, q, v, w, x, y, or z, except where they occur in words derived from English. The compounds "mh" and "bh" give a v/w sound, while "dh" represents a j/y sound. In the 2016 census, almost 1.8 million Irish citizens reported that they speak Irish, with 73,000 people speaking it on a daily basis.

On **March 21, 2009**, the Irish rugby union team won the Six Nations Championship, along with a coveted Grand Slam, when they defeated Wales in Cardiff's Millennium Stadium. It was the first time they had won the championship since **1985** and the first time they had won the Grand Slam since **1948**. They won the Championship again in **2014** and **2015** and repeated their Grand Slam victory in **2018** on St Patrick's Day at Twickenham, England. They returned home to a hero's welcome.

GOD IS GOOD,
BUT NEVER
DANCE IN A
SMALL BOAT.

IRISH PROVERB

WE CAN BE HEROES

People We Are Proud
to Call Our Own

In the fifth century, **St Patrick** spread the message of Christianity in Ireland. He is said to have used the shamrock—now the iconic symbol that encapsulates the celebrated "luck of the Irish"—to teach pagans about the Holy Trinity. The three leaves represent the Father, the Son, and the Holy Spirit. Meanwhile, Ireland's national symbol, as seen on oversized foam Guinness hats, is the harp. The oldest known harp in existence—dating back to 1300—can be viewed in Trinity College, Dublin.

In July 1967, Belfast girl and astrophysicist **Jocelyn Bell Burnell** noticed a "bit of scruff" on the charts she used to track stars in the skies—she had discovered the first radio pulsars, one of the greatest astronomical milestones of the twentieth century. In 2018, she was awarded the Special Breakthrough Prize in Fundamental Physics for her discovery. Bell Burnell donated the full $3 million prize money to help women, minority and refugee students to become physics researchers.

IRISH MALES
ARE A PIECE OF WORK,
ARE THEY NOT?

Bono

Next time you are watching *The West Wing*, give thanks to Irish architect **James Hoban**, for it was he who designed the White House. After emigrating to the US in 1785, Hoban won a design competition for the White House in July 1792 (although the West Wing and the Oval Office were, in fact, later additions).

County Mayo-born **Mary Robinson** is a modern national icon. In 1990, she became the seventh president of Ireland, but more importantly she became the country's first female president. She is widely considered to have transformed and revitalized the role of president during her seven-year tenure.

I was elected by the
women of Ireland,
who instead of
rocking the cradle,
rocked the system.

MARY ROBINSON

Becky Lynch, born Rebecca Quin in January 1987, has brought Ireland to the forefront of professional wrestling. Dubbing herself "The Man," she is a four-time women's champion in World Wrestling Entertainment (WWE). In 2019, she won both the Raw Women's Championship and the SmackDown Women's Championships, making her the only woman ever to hold both titles simultaneously. It was also the first time a WrestleMania event was headlined by women.

Born in County Kildare, **Ernest Shackleton** was one of the world's great explorers and a leading figure in the so-called "Heroic Age of Antarctic Exploration." In January 1909, Shackleton and his team travelled further south than anyone had managed up to that point. The journey, detailed in his book, *The Heart of the Antarctic*, was treacherous, and he was knighted by King Edward VII upon his triumphant return. Several years later Shackleton led another Antarctic expedition, but his ship was crushed and sank in the pack ice. He led his men to a nearby island, and from there set out in a tiny life boat with a small crew across 800 miles of rough ocean to seek help. His incredible rescue mission was a success.

Born and raised in Holywood, County Down, golfer **Rory McIlroy** is one of the most thrilling players to have achieved major success. A four-time major champion, he won the US Open in 2011, the PGA Championship in 2012, the Open Championship in 2014, and the PGA Championship again in 2014. McIlroy is reportedly worth more than $150 million through a combination of winnings and mega-sponsorship deals and has twice been named RTÉ Sports Person of the Year. Go Rory!

IT'S NOT THAT THE IRISH ARE CYNICAL. IT'S RATHER THAT THEY HAVE A WONDERFUL LACK OF RESPECT FOR EVERYTHING AND EVERYBODY.

Brendan Behan

World champion boxer **Katie Taylor** is one of only seven boxers in history, female or male, to hold all four major world titles simultaneously— the WBA, WBC, IBF, and WBO. In 2019, Taylor was ranked best active female lightweight and number one pound-for-pound boxer in the world. Hugely popular in Ireland and the US, the Bray bruiser was flag-bearer for Ireland at the 2012 London Olympics, going on to win Olympic gold. Taylor was invited to the White House in 2010 and is the subject of the 2018 documentary *Katie*. Beat that!

AN IRISHMAN CAN
BE WORRIED BY THE
CONSCIOUSNESS THAT
THERE IS NOTHING TO
WORRY ABOUT.

AUSTIN O'MALLEY

SOMETHING TO REMEMBER US BY

Our Nation's
Cultural Highlights

Located in the beautiful Boyne Valley, the prehistoric monument at **Newgrange** in County Meath is a one-acre mound believed to have been constructed over 5,000 years ago (around 3200 BC), making it older than Stonehenge and the Great Pyramid of Giza. The passage tomb is thought to have had some kind of religious significance, and it features many examples of Neolithic art.

THE HEART OF
AN IRISHMAN IS
NOTHING BUT
HIS IMAGINATION.

George Bernard Shaw

The **Ring of Kerry**, on the Iveragh
Peninsula, is a beautiful 179-kilometer
(112-mile) circular tourist route around
County Kerry in south-west Ireland. It
encapsulates everything the world loves
about Ireland—mighty castles, high
cliffs, ancient monuments, spectacular
landscapes carved out of ancient glaciers,
and famous archaeological treasures.
It even has some of Europe's
best unspoiled beaches.

The sound of Irish
seems to be locked
in the subconscious
mind of our people.

KATE FENNELL

At their highest, the craggy **Cliffs of Moher** in County Clare stand at a massive 214 meters (702 feet) and stretch for 8 kilometers (5 miles) along the Atlantic Ocean. On a clear day, you can see the Aran Islands and Galway Bay, as well as the famous Dingle Peninsula. Over a million tourists visit the area every year—just don't get too close to the edge!

Northern Ireland's most famous natural highlight, the **Giant's Causeway** is a coastal area of around 40,000 basalt columns near Bushmills, County Antrim—near where the famous Bushmills Irish whiskey is distilled. Legend tells of a giant called Finn McCool who created the causeway of stones to scare off a rival Scottish giant. In fact, they were created by a volcanic eruption some 60 million years ago.

Visiting the enthralling **Aran Islands**
is like stepping back in time. Situated
on the west coast, in Galway Bay, the
three remote islands of Inishmore,
Inishmaan, and Inisheer are famed
for their geological formation
as well as their preservation of a
rural human existence that has
remained unchanged for centuries.
If you go, expect to speak Irish.

**AN IRISHMAN WAS
ASKED IF THE IRISH
ALWAYS ANSWERED ONE
QUESTION WITH ANOTHER.
"WHO TOLD YOU THAT?"
HE REPLIED.**

Niall Toíbín

Dublin's most compulsory cultural highlight, the legendary **Guinness Storehouse** tells the story of how Ireland's proud national drink came to be the country's largest export. Designed around an atrium shaped like a massive pint glass, the building has seven floors dedicated to Guinness history. The Gravity Bar, on the top floor, has cracking views of Dublin, too. Over a million visitors now stop by each year, many of them having a cheeky one for the road.

The mighty **Burren** in County Clare, around 250 square kilometers (97 square miles) in size, is a giant rocky surface made up of limestone karst plates. In the summer it is populated by around 700 different plant species, including 22 of Ireland's 27 native orchids. A sight to behold from the air, it derives its name from the Irish *Boíreann*, a rocky place. An astonishing three quarters of all of Ireland's native plant species grow in the Burren, so tread carefully if you decide to take a wander.

Every year, over three million people visit Ireland's national (and largest) church, **St Patrick's Cathedral** in Dublin. The current building was largely erected in the thirteenth century, but St Patrick is believed to have baptized people into Christianity on this very site 800 years before that. The cathedral is also revered as the first place Handel's *Messiah* was performed, in 1742.

Ireland's two national sports, hurling and Gaelic football, are played at Dublin's **Croke Park** stadium, a sacred spiritual home for both sports. With capacity for 82,300 spectators, it is the third largest stadium in Europe—a massive achievement considering hurling and Gaelic football are still amateur sports. Croke Park is the headquarters of the Gaelic Athletic Association (GAA).

After you've followed in the footsteps
of giants at the Causeway, why not
walk a couple of miles down the
road to the oldest licensed whiskey
distillery in Ireland—**Old Bushmills**.
Visited by over 100,000 Irish whiskey
fans each year, the distillery is also
the oldest working whiskey maker
in the world, dating back to 1608.

WE ARE ALL
IN THE GUTTER,
BUT SOME OF US
ARE LOOKING AT
THE STARS.

OSCAR WILDE

STARS IN OUR EYES

The Entertainers
We Love

Irish dance sensation **Riverdance** celebrated its twenty-fifth anniversary in 2020. Since opening in Dublin in February 1995, the stage show has been seen by over 25 million people in 450 venues worldwide, making it one of the most successful dance shows in the world. Riverdance's unique formula combines traditional Irish music and dance. "Riverdance is as much a phenomenon as a show," wrote the *New York Post*.

THE IRISH, AND
I'M GUILTY OF THIS,
THINK THEY INVENTED
EVERYTHING.

Bono

Since forming in 1976, **U2** have gone on to become one of the world's biggest rock bands, releasing more than a dozen studio albums and racking up a record 22 Grammy Awards. In the 1990s they were Ireland's biggest export, above potatoes and Guinness! Noteworthy in such a fickle industry is the fact that the original line-up remains: singer Bono, guitarist The Edge, bassist Adam Clayton, and drummer Larry Mullen, Jr. Bono is the only person ever to be nominated for a Grammy, an Oscar, a Golden Globe, and the Nobel Peace Prize.

Saoirse Ronan is an Irish-American actress who is steadily establishing herself as an acclaimed Hollywood star. After developing a name in period dramas, in recent years she received critical acclaim for her roles in *Brooklyn*, *Lady Bird*, and *Little Women*. Born in the Bronx and raised in Dublin, Ronan won a Golden Globe Award in 2018 for *Lady Bird*. In addition to her acting talents, she is vocal about equality and women's rights.

Belfast-born **Sir Kenneth Branagh**
is a legend of the stage and the silver
screen, with a successful career in
acting and directing under his belt.
Branagh has been nominated for five
Academy Awards and five Golden
Globes, and he has three BAFTAs
and two Emmys to his name. He
earned acclaim for his Shakespeare
adaptations but has starred in roles
as diverse as Ernest Shackleton, Victor
Frankenstein, Franklin D. Roosevelt,
and Hercule Poirot. He was made
a Freeman of Belfast in 2018.

Ireland was a
place for the renewal
of hope and I still
see it like that.

DANIEL DAY-LEWIS

Mary Black is a national treasure
and quite possibly *the* voice of Ireland.
Born in Dublin, Black is a popular folk
and Celtic singer whose voice is purer than
snow and very bewitching. She has sung
traditional and contemporary Irish
songs since the age of eight.

Dubliner **Phil Lynott** rose to
international fame as the charismatic
frontman of 1970s Irish rock legends
Thin Lizzy. The band went on to achieve
major international success with hits
including "The Boys Are Back in Town"
and "Jailbreak." The singer, songwriter
and bassist died in 1986 at the age of
36 after a lengthy struggle with drug
addiction. A statue was erected in his
memory in Dublin in 2005.

**IF YOU'VE GOT
NOTHING BUT A
SENSE OF HUMOR,
YOU WILL SURVIVE.**

Phil Lynott

Qui-Gon Jinn. Ra's al Ghul. "Hannibal" Smith. Michael Collins. Oskar Schindler. Aslan the Lion. Zeus. Bad Cop/Good Cop. These are just a handful of the characters whose portrayal has propelled **Liam Neeson** into being one of the biggest Irish actors on the international stage. He was nominated for the Best Actor Oscar for his role in *Schindler's List* in 1993 and he was added to the Hollywood Walk of Fame in 2014. In 2018, Irish President Michael D. Higgins honored Neeson with an award for his "contribution to humanity." Not bad for a lad from Ballymena.

The feisty redhead **Maureen O'Hara** was one of the stars of the Golden Age of Hollywood, earning herself the title "The Queen of Technicolor." O'Hara, from Dublin, was best known for her roles starring alongside John Wayne and working with director John Ford in a career that spanned 50 years. She was presented with an Honorary Academy Award in 2014 and passed away in 2015.

Brian, Nicky, Kian, Mark, and Shane were boy band **Westlife**, Ireland's most prolific chart-toppers. Over a period of 14 years the band sold over 45 million records worldwide and were the first act in history to have their first seven singles all reach Number One in the charts. Their debut single "Swear It Again" sold over 365,000 copies, a record at the time. After Brian left the group, they continued entertaining millions until 2012, and the four-piece later reformed in 2018.

He may look perma-grumpy but **Van Morrison** has a lot to smile about. Born in Belfast, Van the Man is a Grammy-award-winning music legend. By 2011, Morrison's 1967 hit "Brown Eyed Girl" joined an elite group of just ten songs that had been played on US radio ten million times—an average of 225 times a day for 44 years! It remains the most played and downloaded song from the 1960s.

BEING IRISH
IS VERY MUCH
A PART OF WHO I
AM. I TAKE IT
EVERYWHERE
WITH ME.

COLIN FARRELL

Born in Dublin in 1951, **Bob Geldof** is now as much a part of the Irish furniture as the Blarney Stone. The lead singer of The Boomtown Rats became a household name around the world as the co-writer of the charity single "Do They Know It's Christmas?" in 1984 and organizer of the *Live Aid* charity concert in 1985. He infamously swore live on TV during the event, highlighting his fierce passion for the cause to end the Ethiopian famine crisis. It prompted millions of people to phone in.

British-made sitcom *Father Ted* is one of the best-loved comedy series in Irish TV history. Starring an Irish cast including Dermot Morgan, Ardal O'Hanlon, and Pauline McLynn, it follows the trials, tribulations, and misadventures of three Irish priests, Ted, Dougal, and Jack, who share a rectory on the fictional Craggy Island off Ireland's west coast. Mrs Doyle, their housekeeper, always wants to serve them tea. Notable fans of the show include Steven Spielberg, Madonna, Steve Martin, Jim Carrey, and Cher.

THE WRITE STUFF

Famous Writers,
Poets and Playwrights

Marian Keyes is one of the most successful Irish novelists of all time. Her novels are worldwide bestsellers, with over 30 million books sold in 33 languages. Keyes tackles many facets of modern life and relationships, exploring issues such as addiction and depression, all with her trademark wit. Among her hobbies she includes reading, movies, shoes, handbags, feminism, and cake. She is known for her charity work. We love you, Marian!

OPTIMISM
CAN BE
RELEARNT.

Marian Keyes

Belfast-born **C. S. Lewis** is best remembered for the seven classic fantasy tales within *The Chronicles of Narnia*, beginning with the much-loved *The Lion, The Witch and The Wardrobe*. Published between 1949 and 1954, the adventures of Aslan, the Pevensie children, and many other beloved characters have sold over 100 million copies and been adapted numerous times for radio, stage, television, and film.

The 1897 gothic masterpiece
Dracula introduced the world to
the frightening otherworldly horrors
of blood-drinking vampire Count Dracula
and vampire-hunter Van Helsing. But
the novel also made famous the Irish
writer **Bram Stoker**, who was born in
Clontarf, Dublin, in 1847.

We learn
from failure,
not from
success.

BRAM STOKER

Every university student's favorite Irish poet, and winner of the 1995 Nobel Prize for Literature, **Seamus Heaney** was a professor at Harvard University for 16 years. Considered one of the most revered Irish poets since W. B. Yeats, his first collection of poetry, *Death of a Naturalist,* was published in 1966. Heaney died in August 2013, and the nation mourned.

This century has seen the extraordinary success of Irish female authors. Between them, **Anna Burns**, **Anne Enright**, **Eimear McBride**, **Sarah Crossan**, **Sally Rooney**, **Maggie O'Farrell**, and **Emma Donoghue** have won multiple major awards, including the Booker Prize (Burns and Enright), the Baileys Women's Prize for Fiction (McBride), the Goldsmiths Prize (McBride), the Carnegie Medal (Crossan), the Costa Book Award (Rooney and O'Farrell), and the Stonewall Book Award (Donoghue). The boys haven't done too badly for themselves either: successful contemporary male writers include **Sebastian Barry**, **Joseph O'Connor**, **John Boyne**, and **Roddy Doyle**.

Seventy years ago, **Samuel Beckett** wrote one of his many literary masterpieces, *Waiting for Godot*, an absurdist play featuring two characters, Vladimir and Estragon, endlessly waiting for someone called Godot to arrive. The drama has been named the most significant English-language play of the twentieth century by the National Theatre of Great Britain. Beckett, from Foxrock, Dublin, won the Nobel Prize for Literature in 1969.

Having sold more than 40 million copies of her 16 published novels, the late **Maeve Binchy** is one of Ireland's most popular female writers—and her success made her one of the country's richest women. Her first book, *Light a Penny Candle* (1982), received at the time the largest ever advance sum for a first novel—£52,000.

IN IRELAND EVERY PLACE
YOU VISIT AND EVERY
PERSON YOU MEET
HAS A STORY ...
YOU WILL NEVER
BE BORED.

Maeve Binchy

Born in Dublin on October 16, 1854,
Oscar Wilde was as flamboyant as he
was intelligent. A cunning linguist as
well as a master of wit, wordplay, and
acute observations on social class, he
wrote enduring plays, poems, and prose.
Wilde's last witticisms were always
going to be fabulous. He is said to
have remarked on his deathbed: "My
wallpaper and I are fighting a duel to
the death. One or other of us has got
to go!" Truly one of Ireland's sons.

IRELAND IS RICH
IN LITERATURE
THAT UNDERSTANDS
A SOUL'S YEARNINGS,
AND DANCING
THAT UNDERSTANDS
A HAPPY HEART.

MARGARET JACKSON

Born in 1930, **Edna O'Brien** is a celebrated Irish novelist, playwright, and poet known for her courage in tackling taboo subjects. Her first novel, *The Country Girls* (1960), was groundbreaking at the time, exploring the difficulties women faced during a repressive period in Ireland. The book was burned, banned, and denounced from the pulpit. O'Brien's awards include the 2011 Frank O'Connor International Short Story Award. Her memoir *Country Girl* was published in 2012.

William Butler Yeats was the first—but by no means the last—Irishman to win the Nobel Prize for Literature. Honored in 1923, Yeats is the much-loved grandaddy of Irish poetry and a leading figure of twentieth-century literature. He famously used his Nobel Prize as a way to express his proud Irishness: "I consider that this honor has come to me less as an individual than as a representative of Irish literature."

OF OUR CONFLICTS
WITH OTHERS
WE MAKE RHETORIC;
OF OUR CONFLICTS
WITH OURSELVES
WE MAKE POETRY.

W. B. Yeats

Dubliner **George Bernard Shaw** has gone down in history as the only writer to win a Nobel Prize (1925) and an Oscar (1938), the former for his outstanding contribution to literature, the latter for his own screen adaptation of his outstanding play, *Pygmalion*. The screenplay for *Pygmalion* was later adapted into a hugely successful musical, *My Fair Lady*, which you might have heard of. Shaw also founded the London School of Economics, just in case you weren't impressed enough by him already.

Ireland, sir, for good
or evil, is like no other
place under heaven,
and no man can touch
its sod or breathe its
air without becoming
better or worse.

GEORGE BERNARD SHAW

And then there's Joyce. **James Joyce** to be precise. This most distinguished of Irish writers, famous for his avant-garde literary techniques, such as stream of consciousness, was born in Dublin in 1882 and is best known for his 1922 masterpiece *Ulysses*, as well as *A Portrait of the Artist as a Young Man* (1916) and *Finnegans Wake* (1939). If you've managed to finish *Ulysses*, you deserve a prize!

**FUNERALS IN IRELAND
ARE SO JOLLY,
THEY SHOULD BE
CALLED FUNFERALLS.**

James Joyce

FOOD FOR THOUGHT

Our Landmark Dishes

Tayto potato chips are a cultural phenomenon across the whole of Ireland. Not only that, but it was Tayto that *invented* the flavored chip production process, and they were the first to put cooked flavored chips in a bag. When owner Joe "Spud" Murphy set up shop with the Tayto company in 1954, they sold 347 packs of their crisps a day. Now they sell 525 packs a minute!

IF IT WAS
RAINING SOUP,
THE IRISH
WOULD GO OUT
WITH FORKS.

BRENDAN BEHAN

The **Ulster fry** is the Northern Irish equivalent to the full English breakfast, with as many of the following as you can fit onto one plate: Irish bacon, sausages, eggs, potato bread, fried tomatoes, and soda farls. Not as healthy as a banana, but ten times tastier.

On a long, cold night, the perfect
nightcap—sipped all over the world—is
an Irish coffee: hot, strong, black coffee,
a pleasing quantity of **Irish whiskey**
(the particular brand is down to you),
a spoonful of brown sugar, topped off
with thick cream (never whipped).
Designed to leave you with a thick
creamy moustache, an Irish coffee is
always the best way to end an evening.
Or start the day—we won't judge!

ONLY IRISH COFFEE
PROVIDES IN A SINGLE
GLASS ALL FOUR ESSENTIAL
FOOD GROUPS: ALCOHOL,
CAFFEINE, SUGAR AND FAT.

Alex Levine

"**Pooh bear**" is a popular Northern Irish dessert that will hopefully one day cross the Atlantic. Take a few scoops of your favorite vanilla ice cream and mix together with big honeycomb chunks sourced fresh from local bees. Sounds great, doesn't it?

The traditional dish
colcannon warms the soul of
any Irish person, big or small. Mashed
potato and kale or cabbage mixed together
with salt, pepper and butter—nothing else
and nothing more. If you can sprinkle
some shamrocks over the top as the
perfect garnish, then great—you've
got the true taste of Ireland
on your plate.

THAT'S THE
IRISH PEOPLE ALL
OVER—THEY TREAT A
SERIOUS THING AS
A JOKE AND A JOKE
AS A SERIOUS THING.

SEÁN O'CASEY

Food for Thought

Take some bread and boil it in milk.
Add some sugar and cinnamon.
Then brown the dish in the oven.
And there you have it—you've got a
goody. Add whipped cream just to
be sure of maximum flavor. This is
a festive dish, popular in parts of
Ireland at Christmas and on
St John's Eve (June 23).

Dublin coddle is the Dubliners' weapon of choice to line their stomachs before a heavy night out. Sausages, bacon, onion, and potatoes boiled in beef stock. This will fill the stomach and put a fire in your belly, ready to be doused by plenty of pints of Guinness.

Crubeens are boiled pigs' feet that are nibbled on as a snack. Crubeens were at their most popular in the 1800s when bacon factories in Cork, Waterford, Limerick, Dublin, and Belfast opened up. They are the precursor to modern-day pork scratchings—delicious, salty pig snacks sold at pubs to make you want to drink more!

LAUGHTER IS BRIGHTEST WHERE FOOD IS BEST.

Irish proverb

MAPPING THE NATION

Our Geography
and Weather

IRISH
HURRICANE:
A FLAT CALM
WITH DRIZZLING
RAIN.

ANONYMOUS

The island of Ireland is comprised of two separate (but geographically joined) states: the Republic of Ireland (made up of 26 counties) and Northern Ireland, a constituent part of the United Kingdom (made up of six counties). The population of the Republic of Ireland is around 4.9 million; the population of Northern Ireland, about 1.9 million.

THERE IS NO
LANGUAGE LIKE
THE IRISH FOR
SOOTHING
AND QUIETING.

John Millington Synge

The **River Shannon** is the longest river in Ireland. It divides the west from the east and south and is 360 kilometers (224 miles) long. That's approaching the entire length of the island of Ireland, which is 486 kilometers (302 miles).

Ireland's largest freshwater lake is **Lough Neagh**. It's 392 square kilometers (151 square miles) in surface area and lies in Northern Ireland, supplying 40 percent of Northern Ireland's water. It's also the largest lake by area in the UK and Ireland, covering an area a little bit bigger than the island of Lanai in Hawaii.

Ireland's highest peak is **Mount Carrauntoohil**, 1,039 meters (3,408 feet) above sea level. The mountain is the central peak of the brilliantly named MacGillycuddy's Reeks range in County Kerry, south-west Ireland.

IN IRELAND
THE INEVITABLE
NEVER HAPPENS
AND THE
UNEXPECTED
CONSTANTLY
OCCURS.

JOHN PENTLAND MAHAFFY

The most populated region in Ireland is **Dublin**—the Republic's capital city—with an overall population of around 1.4 million people. Including the Greater Dublin area, the figure is around 2 million, or 40 percent of the Irish population. In Irish, *Dubhlinn* means "black pool." The city is home to four universities and is celebrated as a friendly and multicultural European capital.

Ireland is famous for its **peatland bogs**, which cover 20 percent of the island's land area. Cutting and burning "turf" or peat briquettes for warmth is a well-known practice in Ireland and many an Irish person around the world will think back on the smell of a peat fire with nostalgia. In 2015, the semi-state-run Bord na Móna (Peat Board) announced that the use of Ireland's peat bogs for power generation would be phased out by 2030, in a bid to combat climate change.

**AN IRISHMAN WOULD
HAVE BEEN THE FIRST
TO CLIMB EVEREST
BUT HE RAN OUT
OF SCAFFOLDING.**

Noel Purcell

Powerscourt Waterfall, County Wicklow, is Ireland's tallest, and arguably most beautiful, waterfall. It has a fierce drop of 121 meters (397 feet). Fed by the River Dargle, the waterfall is also close to the famous Great Sugar Loaf hill.

WE MAY HAVE
BAD WEATHER IN
IRELAND, BUT THE
SUN SHINES IN THE
HEARTS OF THE
PEOPLE AND THAT
KEEPS US ALL WARM.

MARIANNE WILLIAMSON

With 11 consonants and 11 vowels, **Muckanaghederdauhaulia** (say that five times fast!) is Ireland's longest place name. It is located in historic County Galway and roughly translates as "ridge shaped like a pig's back between two expanses of briny water."

Dunmore Head at the tip of the
Dingle Peninsula is mainland Ireland's
westernmost point. Galway is Ireland's
westernmost city. Then it's about
1,934 miles (3,113 kilometers) until you
reach North America's easternmost city, St
John's in Newfoundland. Bit far to swim!

**YOU KNOW
IT'S SUMMER
IN IRELAND
WHEN THE RAIN
GETS WARMER.**

Hal Roach

OBJECTS
OF OUR
DESIRE

Iconic Objects
and Famous Inventions

The Irish have given the world much more than just Guinness but, as a place to start, **Guinness** is nonetheless a pretty tasty contribution, not to mention the best-selling alcoholic drink of all time. Concocted by Arthur Guinness in the 1770s, this liquid legend is still created at the Guinness Brewery in Dublin. Over ten million pints of the "black gold" are sold proudly every single day in 150 countries around the world, with over three million pints produced at the brewery each day to meet demand!

Built at the Harland and Wolff
shipyard in Belfast, **RMS** *Titanic*
is the most famous and ill-fated ship
ever to sail from Ireland. Of the estimated
2,224 passengers and crew, more than
1,500 died on April 15, 1912 when she sank
in the Atlantic after striking an iceberg.
It was the luxury ocean liner's maiden
voyage, departing from Southampton
and stopping at Cobh (Queenstown)
en route to New York.

The engineer John Philip Holland, from County Clare, designed the first **submarines** to be commissioned by the navies of the United States and the United Kingdom. They were launched in 1897 and 1901 respectively. His 1878 prototype, *Holland Boat No. 1*, was just 14 feet (4.3 meters) in length and dived to a depth of 12 feet (3.7 meters). It can be seen on display in the Paterson Museum in New Jersey.

LOVE IS
NEVER DEFEATED,
AND I COULD ADD,
THE HISTORY
OF IRELAND
PROVES THAT.

POPE JOHN PAUL II

Born in 1857, the very jolly John Joly, from County Offaly, invented two important things: 1) in 1894, by using his special Joly color process, he refined **color photography**; and 2) he devised the first use of **radiotherapy** for use in cancer treatment in 1914, helping save millions of lives. A toast to John Joly!

THERE'S NO
IRISH ACCENT.
EACH COUNTY
HAS A DIFFERENT ONE.

Seán O'Casey

Made from fermented grain mash, distilled three times and aged longer than three years in wooden casks, **Irish whiskeys** (with an e!) are sipped and savored all around the world. The industry has soared in recent years, going from four distilleries in 2010 to more than 20 in 2020, and that number is set to rise. According to the Irish Whiskey Museum, whiskey originated in Ireland, not Scotland, with the earliest written evidence referring to it as "fire water." In 2019 there were global sales of over 135 million bottles of Irish whiskey, worth $800 million in export value. *Sláinte* to that!

For an
Irishman,
talking is
a dance.

DEBORAH LOVE

The first person to establish
the concept of **"absolute zero"**
—the coldest temperature possible
in the universe—was someone familiar
with the concept of feeling the cold: an
Irishman. Belfast-born physicist William
Thomson, 1st Baron Kelvin, will forever be
remembered in the name given to the unit
measurement used to define absolute
temperatures—a kelvin. Absolute
zero is $-459.67\,°F$ ($-273.15\,°C$),
so quite chilly.

As befits an exposed island, fierce gusts of ocean wind regularly batter every corner and crag of the Irish coast. It's no surprise then that an Irishman, Francis Beaufort, devised the **Beaufort wind force scale**—the internationally recognized measure that defines wind speed. Formulated in 1805, the scale is much more informative than just shouting "It's blowing a hooley out there!"

MY ONE CLAIM TO
ORIGINALITY AMONG
IRISHMEN IS THAT I HAVE
NEVER MADE A SPEECH.

George Moore

The **guillotine** is usually associated with the French, right? What if I told you that this gruesome execution device was actually used in Ireland centuries before the French adopted it? Evidence in support of this claim can be found in a sixteenth-century illustration of a man named Murcod Ballagh being executed with such a machine in Ireland in 1307.

TO ANYONE WITH
A DROP OF IRISH
BLOOD IN THEM
THE LAND THEY
LIVE ON IS LIKE
THEIR MOTHER.

ALEXANDRA RIPLEY

CURIOUSER
AND
CURIOUSER

Peculiar Facts You
Probably Didn't Know

**OUR IRISH BLUNDERS
ARE NEVER BLUNDERS
OF THE HEART.**

Maria Edgeworth

Upon his arrival back in Ireland in 1689, after a trip to Jamaica during which he had observed native people mixing cocoa with water, Irish physician and botanist Hans Sloane is said to have mixed cocoa with milk instead. In doing so, some say he invented, or at least popularized, **chocolate milk**!

The Tippling Act 1735 made it illegal for sellers of alcohol to pursue customers for money owed for drinks given on credit above the value of one shilling. That sounds like a recipe for boozing on the cheap, but the aim was to curb the giving of credit and the unruly behavior of those "tempted to resort too frequently to the houses or shops of the retailers of such liquors, where they often drink to excess, and thereby frequently run into debt, and lay themselves under the temptation of purloining their masters' goods to discharge such debts."

WE DON'T
HAVE ANYTHING
AS URGENT AS
MAÑANA IN
IRELAND.

STUART BANKS

Guinness World Records is now an internationally respected reference book for the planet's greatest and strangest achievements. But its beginnings were far more humble. In 1951, Hugh Beaver, managing director of Guinness Brewery at the time, went out hunting one day in North Slob, County Wexford, and got into an argument about what was the fastest game bird in Europe. Unable to locate the answer, he set about commissioning what would soon become *The Guinness Book of Records*. It took only four years to become a global publishing phenomenon.

Imagine the honor of having an interstate gas station named after you! The **Barack Obama Plaza**, built in 2014, was named in tribute to the former US President, whose maternal great-great-great-grandfather Falmouth Kearney emigrated to the US from Moneygall in 1850. The rest stop on the M7 highway has an Obama visitor center and life-sized statues of Barack and Michelle. Obama visited Moneygall in 2011, delighting locals with his remark: "My name is Barack Obama, of the Moneygall Obamas, and I've come home to find the apostrophe we lost somewhere along the way."

**A SECRET IN DUBLIN
JUST MEANS TELLING
ONE PERSON AT A TIME.**

Ciarán MacGonigal

Early Irish law, often referred to as **Brehon law**, consisted of various statutes that governed everyday life in early medieval Ireland. One edict which may raise an eyebrow and a smile today is the following: "A layman may drink six pints of ale with his dinner but a monk may drink only three. This is so he will not be intoxicated when prayer time arrives."

I'm Irish,
so I'm messing
all the time.
Which means,
I'm having a laugh.
I'm always
making jokes.

SAOIRSE RONAN

Curiouser and Curiouser

The **leprechaun** is a mischievous Irish sprite who makes and mends shoes and enjoys playing practical jokes. Solitary souls, leprechauns are generally bearded and wear coats and hats. They live in moors, forests, and caves and know where the pot of gold is buried at the end of a rainbow. And that's not a word of a lie! After a few pints of Guinness, you may well meet one on your way home!

THERE'S NO PLACE LIKE HOME

Famous Places to See and Things to Do

One of the oldest pubs in Ireland—
and therefore one of the best places
to have a pint of Guinness—
is **The Brazen Head**, located on
the south bank of the River Liffey
in Dublin. This celebrated bar is
claimed to date back to 1198 and is
beloved by all for its lively atmosphere
(especially after a few pints). As James
Joyce once said, "You get a decent
enough do in the Brazen Head."

**IRELAND'S RUINS
ARE HISTORIC EMOTIONS
SURRENDERED TO TIME.**

Horace Sutton

In a small town called Downpatrick, County Down, the remains of the nation's patron saint, **St Patrick**, are believed to lie. They rest in a place of quiet worship in Down Cathedral and are worth a visit if you're nearby in Belfast—the gravesite is only 20 miles away.

The award-winning **Titanic Belfast** has become the second most visited tourist attraction in Northern Ireland since it opened in 2012, on the centenary of the *Titanic*'s launch. In 2016, it was crowned the World's Leading Tourist Attraction at the World Travel Awards, and it has been credited with transforming tourism in Northern Ireland. Shaped like the *Titanic*'s hull, locals have nicknamed it "The Iceberg."

I WENT TO
IRELAND ONCE—
IT WAS A BEAUTIFUL
COUNTRY, AND
BOTH THE WOMEN
AND MEN WERE
GOOD-LOOKING.

JAMES CAGNEY

Irish and Proud of It

One of the more bookish things to do in Dublin is to take a **James Joyce-themed walking tour** of the city. Follow in the famous footsteps of Leopold Bloom and walk the route he takes in the "Lestrygonians" episode of Joyce's masterpiece *Ulysses*. En route, you can also stop off at many of the locations mentioned in the stories in *Dubliners*.

Kissing of the mystical **Blarney Stone** at Blarney Castle, near Cork, is a proud Irish tradition, despite the stone being dubbed the "most unhygienic tourist attraction in the world." As the legend goes, anyone who kisses this stone is endowed with the "gift of the gab" —great eloquence, skill of flattery, wit, and charm—not that the Irish need any more than they already have. Millions of people from around the world have visited this tourist site over the past 200 years.

Take a trip to **Inishbiggle**, a small island off the coast of County Mayo and home to just 18 people in the last census. If you're lucky, you might get to meet the entire population.

**MAY THE ENEMIES
OF IRELAND NEVER
EAT BREAD NOR DRINK
WHISKEY, BUT BE
AFFLICTED WITH
ITCHING WITHOUT
THE BENEFIT OF
SCRATCHING.**

Irish saying

With more than 2,200 clubs, **Gaelic football** is one of Ireland's favorite sports. The top three winners of the GAA All-Ireland Football Championship are Kerry (37 times), Dublin (29), and Galway (9). If you get a ticket to a Kerry–Dublin final at Croke Park you're in for a treat! The GAA now extends to many countries around the world, with 400 international clubs including the Jakarta Dragonflies, the Saigon Gaels, the Sydney Shamrocks, the Arabian Celts, the Kuwait Harps, and the Celtic Cowboys from Texas!

Mistakes
are the
portals of
discovery.

JAMES JOYCE

153

The **Dublin Literary Pub Crawl** is the most famous of all Dublin pub crawls—and that's saying something! As the evening's jovial tour guides take you on a walkabout of many of the city's literary hotspots, they will perform extracts from the finest works of some of Dublin's pre-eminent writers, including Joyce, Beckett, and Wilde.

The town of **Dingle**, at the foot of the Slievanea mountain, is one of the most popular tourist attractions in Ireland. Dingle is alive with Irish culture and character and, because the Dingle Peninsula is the most westerly point of Ireland, visitors are treated to two extreme vistas in one panorama—mountains behind them and 3,000 miles of raging ocean in front of them.

**DO YOU NOT FEEL
THAT THIS ISLAND IS
MOORED ONLY LIGHTLY
TO THE SEABED,
AND MIGHT BE OFF
FOR THE AMERICAS
AT ANY MOMENT?**

Sebastian Barry

Described by Oscar Wilde as a "savage beauty," **Connemara** is, to many, the real emerald in Ireland. Sitting at the very edge of Europe, Connemara is a completely unspoilt landscape. It is also the nation's sporting paradise, a place where you can golf, fish, cycle, walk, horse ride, rock climb, scuba dive, sail, swim, and bog snorkel with the most spectacular views in the country.

Once banned by the British for being too nationalistic, **hurling** is Ireland's oldest (and toughest!) field game, believed to be over 3,000 years old. Each team has 15 players and there are seven officials to keep control of proceedings as players use their hurleys (sticks) in an attempt to launch the sliotar (the small cork ball covered in leather) at breakneck speed between the posts. Catch a game during the February–September season at any one of the 46 GAA stadiums around the country.

IF YOU'RE LUCKY ENOUGH TO BE IRISH, THEN YOU'RE LUCKY ENOUGH.

IRISH SAYING

If you're interested in finding out
more about our books, find us on
Facebook at **Summersdale Publishers**
and follow us on Twitter at
@**Summersdale**.

www.summersdale.com

Image credits

Harp and clover icons on pp.9, 10, 14, 15, 18,
19, 26, 27, 32, 33, 38, 39, 44, 45, 48, 53, 55, 59,
60, 67, 69, 70, 75, 78, 79, 83, 86, 87, 92, 93, 98,
100, 104, 105, 110, 111, 115, 116, 122, 123, 127,
128, 132, 136, 138, 141, 144, 148, 151, 152,
156, 158, 160 © Billy Read/Shutterstock.com
Decorative border and cover image on pp.1, 4,
6, 12, 17, 22, 23, 29, 35, 36, 40, 50, 51, 57, 65,
68, 73, 80, 85, 88, 90, 96, 101, 102, 108, 113,
117, 121, 125, 130, 131, 135, 140, 142, 147,
153, 159 © monkographic/Shutterstock.com